6·16·71

About the Book

A few years back, the great auto race tracks of America resounded with the names of Tony Bettenhausen, Lee Petty, and Bill Vukovich. Now it's Gary Bettenhausen, Richard Petty, and Bill Vukovich, Jr., who thrill fans at Indy, Daytona, and Ontario. These "young lions" of auto racing grew up with the sport as a family tradition. The mistakes and triumphs of the fathers make the sons the racers they are today. In this collection of racing tales well-known automotive writer Ross R. Olney tells of seven hard-charging fathers and sons who have won fame in many kinds of auto racing, from sprint cars, to stock cars, to championship driving. Their stories—some amusing, some tragic—are sure to fascinate fans of the fast cars.

AUTO RACING'S YOUNG LIONS

ROSS R. OLNEY

G.P. Putnam's Sons · New York

To Uncle Charley and Aunt Elsie

Copyright © 1977 by Ross R. Olney
All rights reserved. Published
simultaneously in Canada by Longman
Canada Limited, Toronto.
PRINTED IN THE UNITED STATES OF AMERICA
10 up

Library of Congress Cataloging in Publication Data
Olney, Ross Robert, 1929–
    Auto racing's young lions.
    Includes index.
    SUMMARY: Discusses the racing careers of seven
fathers and sons who have each won fame in many kinds of
auto racing. Includes Bill Vukovich, senior and junior,
Lee and Richard Petty, Tony and Gary Bettenhausen, and
others.
    1. Automobile racing drivers—Biography—Juvenile
literature. [1. Automobile racing drivers] I. Title.
GV1032.A10397   796.7'2'0922   [B]   [920]   76-53824
ISBN 0-399-20579-9
ISBN 0-399-61068-5 lib. bdg.

1961744

CONTENTS

The author would like to thank the following for photos, technical and darkroom help, advice, and anecdotes on the careers of the fathers and sons included in this book, and the fathers and sons themselves for their generous assistance:

J. C. Agajanian, Agajanian Enterprises
Al Bloemker, Indianapolis Motor Speedway
Collene Campbell, Rapid Pace
Bill Dredge, STP Corporation
John Fowler and Joan Kennedy, Firestone Tire and
    Rubber Company
Shav Glick, Los Angeles *Times*
Bart Hagerman, Valvoline Oil
Deke Houlgate, Riverside International Raceway
D. Lynn Justis and Jim Foster, International Speedway
    Corporation
Will Kern, Los Angeles *Times*
Jim Lunt, *National Speed Sport News*
Bob Masson, Goodyear Tire and Rubber Company
Allene McCrary, Norris Industries
Patty Molitor, darkroom technician
Ross D. Olney, photographer and darkroom technician
Bob Russo, Ontario Motor Speedway

and my dad Ross N. Olney, long a racing fan, who contributed to this book in many ways.

PROLOGUE

There have always been many father-son combinations in auto racing.

Rodger Ward, a two-time Indy winner, has a son who races. Jim McElreath, the winner of the inaugural California 500 at the beautiful Ontario Motor Speedway, has a son who drives race cars—sometimes in the same race with Jim. Larry Pearson, the son of NASCAR ace David Pearson, is a race driver. Kyle Petty, Richard Petty's son, has tried competitive driving and likes it. Benny Scott's father was a racer.

The father of the great A. J. Foyt was once a midget car driver, which makes A. J. himself another of auto racing's young lions. Marvin Panch's son Richie has all the promise of becoming a NASCAR star.

Bobby Unser's son, Bobby, Jr., is a bright new star in racing. Coo Coo Marlin's son Sterling races stock cars just as his dad has been doing.

Elliot Forbes-Robinson is the son of E. Forbes Robinson of amateur road racing fame. The father of

Stirling Moss, who became a great Grand Prix champion, was once a British driver of note.

Clark Templeman is a young driver in southern California just now branching out. Few fans of Indy in the fifties and early sixties will ever forget the great Shorty Templeman, Clark's father.

Racing has been good to some of these families, not so good to others. None of them, though, has been through an experience like that of the Sirois family.

The Sirois were a racing family. Frenchy Sirois had been in racing for years as a sometime driver, riding mechanic, and car builder. It was natural for his son to turn to motor racing.

The son's nickname was Jigger, in honor of the famous riding mechanic Jigger Johnson. His real name, though it was seldom used, also rang with racing tradition: it was Leon Duray Sirois. Leon Duray was a famous early driver and a hero of the Sirois family.

Leon Duray "Jigger" Sirois dreamed of winning the Indianapolis Speedway race, as do all young drivers. In 1969 he entered and prepared for the qualification runs.

Qualification trials at Indianapolis narrow the sixty-odd entries to a starting field of thirty-three which run the race. Drivers qualify their cars over four days, though often the field is set after only a couple of days, and the bumping from the field of slower cars by faster ones begins. Only one car is almost completely safe from being bumped: the car that was fastest on the first day of qualifications.

This car becomes the "pole position" car, the inside car in the front row. It leads the field into the race. The driver of the pole car has a guaranteed position in racing; he is sure to be in demand for personal appearances and other lucrative ventures. Next to winning the 500, drivers dream of sitting on the pole.

Sirois's dream of racing at Indy was gradually becoming a reality. He drew first qualifying position for the big race. He would be the very first to try the track. He steered his Caves Buick Special out with confidence, but also with a tingle of fear. He had a solid machine, but it was not the best racer at the track that year. Nor did he have the experience of some of the older drivers.

His four-lap qualification run began late in the afternoon under a darkening sky. The air smelled of rain. Jigger headed into the first turn, and the watching crowd cheered approval.

His run proceeded smoothly, at just the right pace. He was doing a good job on the track, a dangerous one for a new driver.

Down near the fourth turn, the last turn before the long straightaway, the crew and chief mechanic of the qualifying car wait with stopwatches. Their job is to watch the lap times very carefully and to call off the qualification run by waving a yellow flag if they feel the car's speed will not get it into the field. A car has three chances to qualify, and once it is qualified officially, it must stick to its best speed, whatever it is, even if it is later bumped. To wave off or not is a crucial decision for the crew.

Jigger's lap speeds were reasonable, but the crew decided that the average might not hold up for a place in the race. Near the end of the four-lap run they waved the yellow flag and the timing clocks stopped.

Sirois, seeing the yellow flag, pulled into the pits. It was no big deal.

Many racing teams take the first qualification run more or less for practice. They make adjustments on the car and wait for their next chance. The Sirois crew imagined that with a bit more work on the car, Jigger could bring the speed up the next time out. All he had to do was wait until the others had had their chance, possibly even that same day.

But when Jigger Sirois's crew waved off his attempt to qualify, they stopped the only qualification run of the day. As the next car started out on the track the rain began to fall. A downpour continued long into the night and forced the closing of the track and the suspension of any further qualification attempts.

Had Jigger Sirois completed the last few hundred feet of his time trial, he would have been on the pole for the race. His qualification speed would have been the fastest for the day because it was the only one. He would have been the last driver to be bumped. He would have led the field over the starting line for the 1969 Indianapolis 500. But he didn't.

Instant fame and riches had just slipped away from Sirois. That year he did not even make the field at Indy. The Sirois crew had problem after problem with the car for the next couple of weeks, and they never did get it ready enough for another fast run. In fact, Sirois has not done well at Indy since that day. Never once has he made the field for the big race.

This young lion of auto racing is commemorated today with the "Jigger" award given annually by the American Auto Racing Writers and Broadcasters Association to the driver with the worst piece of hard luck.

Of course, many of racing's young lions have fared better. In the following chapters are stories of seven of them and of the racing fathers in whose footsteps they have followed.

Bill Vukovich, Sr., the great "Mad Russian" of the 50s. (*Indianapolis Speedway photo*)

1 VUKOVICH

The Mad Russian, they called him, and he fit the picture. From Fresno, California, Bill Vukovich, Sr., raced up through the smaller tracks to reach for the stars at Indianapolis. In 1952 he barely lost the Indy race. He won two others before the track took its toll.

The setting was dramatic for Bill Vukovich's qualifying run for the 1953 Indianapolis 500. Dark gray clouds boiled in the sky over the speedway. Thunder rumbled. The air was heavy. Fans were torn between seeking shelter from the imminent cloudburst and staying to watch the drama on the track.

The solitary pearl-gray roadster was hurtling around at tremendous speed, forced by its fanatical driver. The echo from the engine bounced between the grandstands along the straightaway as he buzzed around the sweeping first turn.

In the cockpit Bill Vukovich stared straight ahead. He knew he was pushing the car to the limit of control, but so what? The car would either take it, or it would break, and that was what it was all about. Anything less than winning was losing, as far as Vukovich was concerned. Whenever he lost, he would kick the car that had let him down, and mechanics knew to avoid him then.

Two years before, in 1951, he had dropped out of the famous five-hundred-mile race after only twenty-nine laps. Then he was just another rookie who had failed, and his departure from the race went almost unnoticed. He boiled with anger. He came back in 1952. He was winning the race when a small part failed. He ended up parked against the third-turn wall, only twenty miles short of the checkered flag.

The 1952 debacle had eaten at his insides all year long. In 1953 he was going to show them.

It began to rain. A crack of thunder exploded over the track, and the rain fell harder.

This was the last of his four qualification laps, and he knew that he had a good run going. He could slow down a little and still make the field for 1953—a wet track is extremely dangerous. But he danced the car through the fourth turn on the last lap, his foot down on the gas as hard as ever. The rain stung his face and blurred his vision. In the stands soaked fans stood awed as the gray roadster rocketed by on a crystal sheet.

At 180 miles per hour the car streaked through the torrents. This was the driver's doing; he had purposely delayed his qualification run until the air was heavy with moisture from the impending rain, in hopes that his engine might yield up a trace more horsepower. He knew that his timing had been nearly perfect.

Vukovich pressed down on the gas in spite of the torrential rain. If he couldn't see ahead, so what? He could see the walls blurring by on each side. If the tires were lifting up on a slick film of water, so what? By then he could aim the car at the finish line and just slide home.

In the cockpit he was grinning. As he splashed under the checkered flag he knew he had set a new record speed.

That was the way Bill Vukovich, Sr., drove.

The 1955 Indy 500 was a race of stars. It was also the last race sanctioned by the American Automobile Association, in part because of what happened that day.

Few in the stands had any doubt that the great Mad Russian, Bill Vukovich, would win. He had won in 1954 and in 1953, and in 1952 he would have won, except for that small part failure at the very end of the race. Jack McGrath would challenge hard, but Vukie would probably win.

Dawn that race morning was dirty gray. Heavy clouds hung low over the great speedway. It was cold in the garages and pits, and the stands seemed to fill more slowly than usual. It was an ominous morning, and some of the drivers felt strangely depressed.

The starting ceremonies concluded under menacing skies, and the field growled into motion. Gasoline and nitro fumes spiked the heavy air as the racers ambled behind the pace car. You could sense the tension of the

Bill Vukovich, Sr., in Victory Lane at the Indianapolis Motor Speedway after his second straight victory. He died trying for his third. *(Indianapolis Speedway photo)*

battle to come. Both McGrath and Vukovich had been flirting with disaster all month long in an effort to be fastest, though now Jack McGrath had out-qualified Vukie and earned a spot in the front row. They were the two to beat. Others would have to battle for third place.

For the first fifty laps it was one of the finest races ever seen at the track. First it was McGrath and Vukie, then Vukie and McGrath, then McGrath leading Vukie again. Neither man would yield. Both were pulling away from the field, first nose to tail, then side by side.

Then McGrath's engine gave out. With a heavy trail of smoke he pulled into his pit, crawled out of his racer, and looked at his dying engine in disgust. "I've got the worst mechanic in the business," he snarled, meaning himself, since he served as his own chief mechanic. He pushed the car to the garage in back of the pits.

On the track Vukie screamed by. He made no gesture to acknowledge that his chief adversary was out. He merely continued to do what he did so well, to step down on the gas and turn left. Now he led the field. Most spectators thought Vukie had his unprecedented third victory in the bag.

It happened on the fifty-seventh lap, after the pit stops, and after the race had settled down to a long, fatiguing grind. Coming off the number-two turn, Rodger Ward's car appeared to be in some trouble—a broken axle, it turned out. Ward fought his out-of-control car as it slammed the wall once, skidded, then slammed again. Next in line, rookie Al Keller saw the disintegrating Ward car and cut to the inside of the track to avoid the accident. The Ward racer finally slammed into a pedestrian bridge abutment and stopped in the track.

At that moment Keller cut back onto the track. From the rear the next car was Johnny Boyd's. And behind Boyd, hurtling out of turn two at high speed, was Vukovich. Boyd tried to cut to the outside to miss the oncoming Keller and the wrecked Ward car. And just at that second Vukie roared onto the scene. The champ took it in instantly. He had no chance at all to go inside, but there was another way—there was still a hole between Boyd's car and the outside wall. He might just make it if he kept his foot on the gas.

At that same instant the Keller car hit the Boyd car. It went spinning toward the outside wall. The hole closed.

The crowd screamed at Vukie to stop, but he couldn't hear. His car slammed Boyd's car, vaulted into the air over the wall, did a lazy end-over-end twist, bounced off some parked cars and the same bridge abutment and crashed upside down in flames outside the track. . . .

Bill Vukovich, Jr., is taller and better looking than his father was. He is more open; he smiles more often. Maybe he enjoys being a race driver more than his father did. "I looked upon him first as my *dad*," he said, "and second as a race driver. I don't think he wanted me to drive." Bill, Jr., was only eleven years old on that day at Indy in 1955.

"He was a superstar," says the son. "So far I haven't

Bill Vukovich, Jr., moments before an Indy race. *(Author)*

shown that quality. When people see me race they compare my record with his. There's no comparison. But if my name was Smith, my record would be better than most."

Bill Dredge, a racing expert, says, "The elder Vukovich was one of the fanatics of racing, ranking with the great Europeans like Tazio Nuvolari, who raced flat out, sick or well, young or old, tired or fresh, drunk or sober." That kind of performance and attitude you can hardly expect a son to duplicate.

But Bill Vukovich, Jr., is trying. . . .

The sun had set and a chill was creeping over the dusty little midget racetrack in central California. The skimpy stands were nearly filled by the few hundred fans gathered. Eager drivers pulled on helmets and prepared for the feature race of the evening. They were not big-name drivers, but that made them even more eager to win.

Wandering about in the pits was a man wearing a white cowboy hat and high-heeled boots. The hat had a band of pheasant feathers and was obviously expensive. The man was J. C. Agajanian, long a wealthy racing promoter and successful car owner. He seemed to have a magic touch in selecting new young drivers: the list of drivers he had hired made up a who's who of big-time automobile racing. On that cool night outside Bakersfield in 1967 he was selecting his next driver, and he had his eye on Bill Vukovich, Jr.

This driver naturally wanted to win the race and

impress the flamboyant Agajanian. Being hired would mean an almost instant leap from dangerous little tracks with small purses to dangerous big tracks—and a chance at fame and fortune. It would mean going from homemade, small-budget equipment, put together in small garages, to the best cars on the market and the finest mechanics to keep them running at top speed.

The midget race began on the darkening track, and Vukovich charged as hard as he could and still keep control. One car flew into the second turn much too fast, flipped, and caromed into the grandstands. Fortunately nobody was sitting where he landed, and the driver was only stunned by the ferocious crash.

Meanwhile, Vukovich charged on.

In the grandstands, the older fans saw more than just a young driver keeping his speeding midget racer at the knife-edge of control. They were also seeing the vision of his father from the past, and so, perhaps, was Agajanian, as through narrowed eyes he watched the race and the racer.

Agajanian watched carefully as Bill Vukovich, Jr., moved up from his mid-pack starting spot. Agajanian had often seen Bill, Sr., race; he watched for the father's skills in the son. So did the older fans there in California.

In the bounding midget race car, Bill Vukovich knew that he didn't have to win the race in order to get the job with Aggie; Agajanian didn't make a judgment on the basis of one race alone. Still, as with his father before him, winning was everything to the son, and losing was

Bill Vukovich, Jr., ready for the mid-California midget race where he attracted the attention of J. C. Agajanian, in rear, wearing white hat. *(Author)*

nothing. A final victory before the local fans at the little track would put the icing on the cake.

By the middle of the backstretch on the first lap, ignoring the car wrecked in the grandstands, jerking the wheel to control the broadsliding back wheels of the racer, he had moved up five spots. On lap two, after the wreckage had been cleared away, he moved up five more and buzzed into the lead.

It was easy for the fans in the stands to span the fifteen years, to drift back. The kid was not a Mad Russian, but he was good. Nobody could ever be a Mad Russian again, but the son had the qualities that make a winner. Maybe he had one thing his dad never had: Bill Vukovich, Jr., knew when to charge and when to back off and wait.

Gradually young Vukovich began to lap the tailenders, to pass them for the second time on the small track.

Then, trouble!

One of the tailenders bumped him into the board wall—an accident, perhaps. The Vukovich car bounced wildly, caroming from the wall and skidding almost sideways on the track.

Racers rushed past all around as Vukovich fought for control. When he finally managed to aim the car in the proper direction, he was in last place.

In the pits, Agajanian smiled with relief. He'd seen it all before. It didn't matter that his favored driver was losing, just so nobody was hurt; he carried the weight of hurt drivers heavily. He already knew he wanted Vukovich in his car at Indy.

But in the cockpit, cold rage settled over the young driver. He'd show them. With caution thrown to the winds, he broadslided the midget on the track until smoke boiled up from straining tires. The fans could smell the burning rubber up in the grandstands. Vukovich was partly sliding down the short main and back stretches, and around both turns he was four-wheel drifting in an effort to catch up.

He was doing it, too. Gradually he began to pass those same tailenders, and then the middle runners in the pack. With only five laps to go he burst into the lead once again.

More trouble! With less than one lap to go, a tire failed, perhaps weakened by contact with the wall and by the sustained charge. The car lurched and began to slide out of control. Battling the wheel, the driver fought on toward the finish line.

The checkered flag dropped, and he limped to a halt only a few yards farther down the track. The crowd was screaming. They had seen the Mad Russian drive again.

The Russian faded and the son took over. He bounded happily from the cockpit and, waving and smiling, accepted the cheers of the crowd. He wiggled off his helmet, brushed a hand through his hair, then waved again.

The Mad Russian would have abandoned the car and quietly slipped away to the garage.

Agajanian hurried toward the pack of mechanics, photographers, and hangers-on around the racer. He watched as Vukie smiled again and signed programs. Aggie knew that young Vukie's way was better.

In 1970 Bill Vukovich, Jr., was driving for Agajanian. Things were not going well. The team had experienced problem after problem with a brand-new car, and in Vukie's hands it had not yet reached competitive speeds.

Remember how his father drove during that blinding rainstorm in 1953?

Maybe young Vukovich was remembering. With scant time left to qualify for the big race, he left the Agajanian team for a ride in the Sugarripe Prune "Special," an excellent car despite its weird name. Vukie was grim. Time was running out, and the weather was threatening to bring time trials to an end.

He qualified the car in the tenth row for the race. As he was doing it, the sky darkened, and before he completed his four laps, rain began to fall. Bill Vukovich, Jr., didn't slow down.

He may have been thinking of his father.

Thousands and thousands of fans were.

Bill Vukovich, Jr., is correct when he says that his record does not yet compare with that of his father. Few drivers in history compare with the Mad Russian. But the younger Vukovich continues to build an impressive series of top finishes in important national races, including Indy.

Richard Petty, probably the best stock-car driver of all time. *(NASCAR photo)*

2 PETTY

Stock car racing is said to be the most competitive kind of motor racing. If this is true, and if seconds-apart finishes are the rule rather than the exception, it is because of the intense competitive spirit of drivers like Richard Petty.

Richard Lee Petty is a tall, gangling, soft-spoken race car driver from Level Cross, North Carolina. Petty's father Lee was a driver of note—in fact, Lee Petty was the all-time winner in stock car racing until his son came along. It took Richard to break Lee's stronghold on the National Stock Car championship.

Richard Petty won his first race on a balmy summer evening in 1960 at the Charlotte Fairgrounds. He was twenty-two years old and had lost a few races before this night. In the field were Rex White, who later became that year's champion, two stock car hall-of-famers, Joe Weatherly and Ned Jarrett, and his own champion father Lee.

"When everybody else broke, we won," Richard Petty recalls with the modesty he still has, even though he is now a superstar of motor racing.

He raced against his father only a few times during 1960 and 1961.

"He beat me like a drum," says the son. "Daddy raced just like he plays golf, just hard enough to beat you. If he had to lay a fender on you, he would, but if it wasn't necessary, he wouldn't.

"Daddy's probably the smartest driver who ever lived because he did it all himself. He drove, he worked on the car, he called the shots on pit strategy. As far as speed is concerned, he won with inferior equipment."

In 1960 Lee Petty finished sixth in national stock car point standings, and Richard finished second. Then came February 1961 and both men were back at Daytona. During a hundred-lap preliminary race, Richard lost control, spun around, and sailed over the wall. By racing standards the crash was not serious. For two hours the medical people picked glass out of his face while he listened to the 500 on the hospital intercom.

Then the word snapped through: Lee Petty had gone over the wall.

Richard ran over, but by the time he arrived at the crash site his father had been removed to the hospital.

"I ran down the bank and saw what was left of the car. There was blood all over the place and people said he was dead for sure. I thought he was dead, too."

Lee Petty survived the terrible crash, but his career as a driver was over. His left leg had been smashed, and he had broken ribs and other internal injuries. He had lost a lot of blood.

It took six months for Lee Petty to get on crutches. All the time he promised, "I will drive again."

But he always added, "If I don't, you know who will."

Lee Petty never did drive again, but he became boss of one of the most successful racing teams in the history of stock car racing. As boss, he was too busy to drive.

And you know who did.

In 1949 the sport of stock car racing was unstructured. There was no book of rules filled with fine print saying what you could and could not do. Nearly anything that ran was acceptable, and any argument not settled on the pasture track with fender bashing could be settled later with fists at the local bar.

Lee Petty was a good businessman and an excellent mechanic. He thought that what he had done to liven up engines in his own garage could be done to help cars win races. Petty studied this new possibility for making money while having fun. He borrowed a car and entered a race, just to test his theory. Predictably, he was a victim of what modern racers call bammin' 'n' frammin'. Though his theory was correct, he returned a scraped and dented car.

No matter. Insurance companies were none the wiser in those days.

In his own cars, prepared by himself, Lee Petty was runner-up for the National Stock Car Championship in 1949, in third place in 1950, in fourth place in 1951. He placed third in '52, second in '53, and first in '54. By then races were sanctioned by NASCAR (the National

31

Association of Stock Car Auto Racing). In the next seven years he was always in the top six, and twice more he was the champion.

In the late 1950s NASCAR needed a showcase speedway, something to demonstrate that it was indeed the main sanctioning body in stock car racing. It had the top driving stars in this field of racing and wanted the world to know it. NASCAR was ten years old in 1959. Since its head, Bill France, was from Daytona Beach where the whole thing had started, that seemed the logical choice for a site.

Daytona Beach was already important in racing. The city's beach had served as straightaway for many a race and high-speed run. France built a 2.5-mile speedway, named it Daytona International Speedway, and held the inaugural race in February 1959.

The first Daytona 500 had a finish so close that it took three days of examining photos of the finish before the winner could be declared. Officials pondered pictures and sent out calls for more photos, even from nonprofessionals. It was extremely difficult to tell who had won, the two leaders were so close together.

Finally the announcement was made. The winner of the first Daytona 500 was former NASCAR champion Lee Petty, already on his way to another national championship. No man had been National Stock Car Champion more than once, and Petty soon went on to become champion for the *third* time.

In 1959 Richard Petty was twenty-one years old and

32

The first Daytona Speedway finish was so close it took three days to decide the winner. Number 48, Joe Weatherly, is one lap behind. Number 42, Lee Petty, was eventually declared the winner over number 73, Johnny Beauchamp, even though Beauchamp took the trophy in victory ceremonies. *(NASCAR photo)*

just learning to drive on the speedways. The previous year he had been named Rookie of the Year in NASCAR racing.

By 1961 Lee Petty was forty-seven years old. He had had a fine, winning career. He was hurt. He had won fifty-four major races, but time was passing. He had a son who had the talent to carry on, a son who even then was catching up to him and could possibly one day surpass his own stunning records. As of 1975 Richard Petty had been NASCAR champ six times—more often than anyone else—and he had won the Daytona race five times.

Stock cars have changed since Lee Petty first started to race. The cars raced today bear about as much resemblance to the models in dealers' showrooms as Indy cars do to Soap Box Derby racers. They look somewhat alike, and they sometimes have the same names, but that's about it.

Today's stock cars are pure race cars, conceived and built as race cars from the garage floor up.

A body shell, called the body in white, comes into the racing shop. This is the bare skeleton of a car—no interior, windows, exterior trim, paint, or engine. Mechanics remove the doors, then cut the fender wells away to accommodate the wide racing tires. The frame is removed and the body set on chassis rails.

Then comes the most important part of the car's structure, the roll cage. Made from over 250 feet of one-and-three-quarter-inch steel tubing, the roll cage

surrounds and protects the driver. It also helps support the engine and suspension parts. The roll cage is the backbone of a racing stock car. Once the body has been welded to the crosspieces of the roll cage and the doors welded shut, the car is a metal box strong enough to withstand rollovers and end-over-end flips.

Next a racing engine is added, custom heavy-duty suspension is put underneath, and drive train parts, all special racing types, are installed. A gas tank with a special rubber bladder is attached. Heavy-duty brakes (usually disc in the front, drum in the rear) are installed and vented. Special racing wheels, a custom seat molded to the driver's body, and a six-point safety harness are installed along with necessary instruments.

Technically the car remains a Dodge, Ford, Mercury, or Chevrolet, but there is little left of the original automobile. In such hybrid machines Richard Petty, a winner and the son of a winner, has built his remarkable record. There have been plenty of colorful moments along the way.

Darlington had long been Richard Petty's nemesis. This nearly thirty-year-old, one-and-three-eighth-mile speedway in South Carolina is a tough track for every driver. It demands high energy, and it leaves drivers limp. On its narrow, high-banked turns mistakes can be difficult to correct.

In practice for the 1970 Rebel 500, Petty, as if in warning, had slammed the wall. He ripped the rear wing from his Plymouth Super Bird and damaged the car too severely to use again.

"I don't know what happened," he reported later. "I guess I just didn't turn the wheel enough, or maybe I cut a tire."

The Petty crew, under the direction of Lee Petty, called up the reserves. Richard started the Rebel 500 in the backup car, a 1970 Plymouth Roadrunner.

On the 176th turn of the 291-mile race, Petty was battling hard. He approached the infamous turn-four wall, where racers run high and close to the concrete. As a national television audience and forty thousand fans at the track watched, the Petty car, drifting high, slammed hard against the wall, careened across the track to knock a hole in the foot-thick concrete inside wall, then flipped over. All the while the helpless driver's arms flopped wildly out the window (new rules require a safety net over the window to keep arms and head inside). The car bounced end over end and then rolled sideways five times before coming to a smoking halt in the main stretch.

Stunned fans caught their breath. The crash had been one of the most spectacular in all of NASCAR racing. A pall settled over the speedway as the driver was extricated from the wreckage. Petty appeared to be unconscious.

Sometime later the report came from the hospital. The driver had suffered facial cuts and a dislocated shoulder, but he would be back to drive again.

Richard Petty truly believes he can win every race, every time, and he is puzzled and disbelieving when he loses.

Auto Racing's Young Lions

The 1975 Delaware 500 Winston Cup race looked at first like just another Petty victory, a runaway for him on the high-banked one-mile oval of Dover Downs.

On lap ninety-five at the end of a yellow-flag caution period (where speed is reduced), he shot around former leader Dave Marcus and pulled away from the field. His big blue-and-red STP Dodge seemed glued to the fast groove, and he built a substantial lead over Marcus, Richard Brooks, Benny Parsons, and Cale Yarborough.

Meanwhile mechanical problems were hitting other drivers, and debris from collisions and blown engines littered the track. With a safe ten-second lead, nobody else on the same lap, and less than 180 miles left in the race, it almost appeared that Petty could shut down his engine and coast to victory. Even David Pearson, Petty's chief rival, had dropped out with a sour engine.

But in racing things can change in a hurry. Somewhere else in the field Elmo Langley's car exploded, sending a flywheel spinning away from the scene. It came to rest far down the track, unnoticed by corner workers. It also went unnoticed by Richard Petty, who was just beginning to relax and enjoy his Sunday drive.

The sharp steel flywheel bounced up from under Petty's front tire and sliced through a tie rod on the speeding Dodge. For all practical purposes, that should have been the end of the race for Petty. As he limped into his pit, he could barely steer his racer, and spectators assumed it would have to go into the garage area.

But the Petty crew did not push the disabled car into the garage. Instead, they repaired the damage and sent number 43 back into the race. The trouble was that repairing the damage meant replacing the tie rod, and by then Richard was a full eight laps behind.

Cale Yarborough was in the lead with a four-lap advantage over second-place man Dick Brooks. Some said that Petty, who didn't really need to win, was foolish to come back into the race.

The gold-and-white Yarborough car began to slow down with mechanical problems. Helped by some yellow flags and driving steadily, Petty's STP Dodge caught up with the leaders with twenty-nine miles to go in the race. The crowd couldn't believe its eyes. As Yarborough pitted for the final time with his mechanical problems, Petty moved into third place, not too far behind Brooks and Parsons, the leaders. Petty was still almost a full lap behind, but he needed only a bit of luck to help him close the gap in the remaining minutes— and the Petty luck is legend in NASCAR racing. Sure enough, the spin of a back runner brought out still another caution flag. The gap was closed. It was a three-car, one-two-three draft for the finish.

With moments remaining, it was Brooks, Parsons, and then Petty, who not long before had been eight laps behind. Not only does Petty have luck, he also has great skill, coupled with solid determination to win. In the closing seconds of the Delaware 500 Winston Cup race, he rocketed around Brooks, then Parsons. At the checkered flag he was less than one second ahead.

But he was ahead.

Racing expert Bill Dredge tried to explain Richard Petty.

"Richard, more than any other father-son example, has taken the torch directly from his father's hand and gone on to build a racing record that is unequaled in the sport. While I didn't know Lee as a racer, I find it hard to believe that he was as affable, easygoing, seemingly unconcerned, and gentle off the track as Richard is.

"But those who aren't close to Richard can't know that once he is strapped into a race car, he undergoes a remarkable metamorphosis that I have never seen approached by any other racer. It is my personal belief that this total character change while in competition is responsible for the fatigue and other signs of frailty which Petty sometimes evidences."

Dredge leaned forward, warming to his subject. He is a man who loves motor racing, and he loves to talk about it.

"I believe that his concentration on racing and winning is unequaled in the sport. Good as Lee Petty was, and for his time and equipment he was the best in stock cars, Richard Petty has far outstripped his famous father and thus made himself into an almost impossible act for his own son to follow."

Does Petty want his own son to race? Did Lee Petty want Richard to race?

Lee says, "He was interested in cars, and I knew he was going to be a race driver. It was a natural thing for him to do. If I'd been a farmer or a trucker, he would have been a farmer or a trucker. He just did what I did."

Richard says, "Kyle is busy getting the snot kicked out of him trying to play high-school football. But he'll try racing, I'm sure of that. He's just like I was when my daddy was running and I was Kyle's age. He's a pretty good football and basketball player, too. He does as good as he wants to in the classroom, or as bad. If he wants to race, fine, I'll do all I can. If he wants to throw footballs, I'll throw them back as long as I can. But I'd never push him into following me."

Richard Petty does not win every race he enters. The 1976 Daytona 500 is an example of that. But that race also shows that when Petty doesn't win it's not because he doesn't try. Nothing seems to dim his belief that he can win no matter what happens to him or his car.

Petty was leading the 1976 Daytona 500. But a caution flag near the end bunched up the field behind Petty and set up what was certain to be a wild dash for the checkered flag. Soon David "Silver Fox" Pearson, a prime challenger, caught up, and it was Petty and Pearson bumper-to-bumper, battling for the richest victory in NASCAR racing.

Sometimes the man in second place at tracks like Daytona has the advantage, providing he is right on the bumper of the leader. In a phenomenon known as drafting, the second-place car is pulled ahead by the slight vacuum created behind the lead car. When the finish line is a couple of hundred yards ahead, the

second-place car can swing out and around the leader in a sudden burst of speed. This maneuver is called slingshotting, and it is frequently practiced toward the end of Daytona races.

This time, however, it looked as if David Pearson didn't want to draft; he wanted to lead. He pulled around Richard Petty. Perhaps he felt that his car was that much faster than Petty's 43, perhaps he felt that Petty would not be able to get up enough speed to slingshot him.

The cars of Richard Petty (number 43) and David Pearson (number 21) slide into the wall at Daytona at the very end of the race. In a stunning finish both wrecked cars limp slowly over the line, with Pearson a few feet ahead. (*NASCAR photo*)

Rather than attempting to block Pearson's pass, Petty dropped behind, obviously setting up the slingshot.

What fan could have guessed at that moment that he was about to see the slowest finish in Daytona history?

Pushing the gas pedal to the floor, Richard Petty dropped down and started around David Pearson. Pearson was traveling at more than 180 miles per hour. Petty hoped to move a trifle faster.

Then the two cars touched.

Instantly both spun out of control. Pearson's Mercury slammed into the wall, crumpling body metal and shaking the driver like a rag doll. At the same moment, Petty's car smashed into the same wall, parts flying through the air.

From the wall both cars spun down the banked angle of the track into the infield, where clouds of dirt and grass flew from spinning, digging tires. Bent and smoking, the once-beautiful race cars looked like they were ready for the auto graveyard. Inside, each driver shook his head, trying to reorient himself after the wild ride.

But Pearson's engine was still running. Though body parts and radiator were bent into the engine, though coolant was cut off and many electrical and fluid lines severed, the engine still struggled. Just as Pearson realized that he still had a chance to win, Petty's crew arrived at the disabled number 43. They were getting ready to push to get the Petty engine going, though one wheel was at an odd angle and the body was bent and torn. Fans in the stands, worn to a frazzle by the battle, could only stand and stare in shocked amazement as the great race continued.

Pearson edged the jerking and struggling Mercury over the last thirty feet toward the finish line. The engine in the racer was gasping its last and everybody knew it. Even the starter watched with mouth agape and checkered flag hanging limp at his side.

And Petty's car was moving, too, crawling for the line, propelled only by the starter motor.

The two battered and smoking race cars crept over the finish line at less than fifteen miles per hour. David Pearson was ahead.

Richard Petty finished second. But to the great crowd who cheered the incredible finish, both drivers were victors in one of the wildest races of all.

Duane Carter, Sr., during his driving days. Here his arm is held aloft by J. C. Agajanian and a jubilant crew after Carter has qualified for the 1955 Indy race in Aggie's car, number 98. (*Indianapolis Speedway photo*)

3 CARTER

In 1948 a thirty-five-year-old rookie qualified to race in the Indianapolis 500. His starting position for the race was in the next-to-last row, twenty-eighth in the field of thirty-three.

Others in that 1948 race were Rex Mays, Mauri Rose, Ted Horn, Duke Nalon, Tony Bettenhausen, Lee Wallard, and several more drivers then well-known to fans. Then there was the rookie.

The race cars of that era were not the squat, flat, rear-engined machines of today, where the drivers lie almost flat in the cockpit and disappear into the car out of sight of the spectators. These were true open-cockpit racers. The drivers, sitting upright and strapped into padded leather seats, could be seen clearly as they roared by with their arms straight out and elbows locked to help control the unpredictable cars.

This was the era of the Novi Special, a man-killing car that caught the fancy of the fans with its peculiar whining bellow. There was also the odd, six-wheeled Pat Clancy Special. Everybody nearly laughed it off the

Speedway grounds, but it finished in twelfth place that day. In 1948 the winner of this greatest race of all split a purse of only $43,000 with his owner and crew (today the purse is over a million).

The rookie in that 1948 race was not really unknown. In those days, no inexperienced, unknown driver could make it as far as the Speedway. Fans and other drivers mostly knew this rookie as Pappy.

His real name was Duane Carter, and he had all the experience anyone could ask. He had been driving for fourteen years, he was a midget race car champion, he had won major races against some of these same big-name drivers. He was a professional, and his life was racing.

That day Duane Carter lost a wheel and crashed on lap sixty. He had moved from his back-of-the-field starting position to sixth place. Even with his crash, he managed an eleventh-place finish. Not bad for a rookie. Not bad for anybody.

Duane Carter never won an Indy race. But the 1948 race started a long string of 500s for him that did not end until 1964. Carter became one of the best known and most sought after of all the top drivers. He could be counted on to give a car the best drive possible, every time without fail. He was smooth, consistent, and polished.

Racing was good to Duane Carter, offering him a life of financial security and fame. Carter was good for auto racing: he lectured on safety, raced with devotion and sportsmanship, and created an image of professionalism.

Duane Carter, Sr., has a racing family. He was one of the best drivers of all in an earlier era. Silver-haired and handsome today, he stands out in the pits of his son Duane, Jr., his younger son Dana, and his stepson Johnny Parsons.

Duane Carter, Jr., sometimes known as Pancho, is the first driver in racing history to win both a National Midget Championship and a National Sprint Car Championship. He was the only USAC driver ever to finish in the top ten in four racing divisions— championship, midget, sprint, and stock cars. He was Rookie of the Year at Indianapolis in 1974, and racing experts were predicting that Pancho Carter was the first driver to come along who might eventually be better than A. J. Foyt himself. Many young drivers were good, but Pancho seemed better.

When the Indianapolis *Star* asked him why he was so good, he replied, "A combination of things. Mainly, being around racing so long and paying attention. I've also been able to adapt pretty well, and that probably came from driving TQ's (three-quarter midget racers) when I was real young, plus having some natural ability."

"I drive as hard as I can every time I get in a race car," states Pancho Carter. "I think my dad is glad I chose motor racing as a career because I'm sure he loves racing as I do."

Of the kinds of racing at which the Carters excel, sprint racing is the most dangerous. Sprint racers are open-cockpit, open-wheeled cars driven on dirt tracks. From spinning rear wheels flare the great fans of dirt clods that so appeal to followers of this type of racing. When the wheels of two racing sprint cars touch, one car generally rebounds away, sometimes crashing through the fence. Often the other car flips out of control as well. Yet wheel-to-wheel racing is the rule with sprint cars. It is wild, spectacular racing indeed.

The dirt track at Terre Haute, Indiana, has always been the scene of exciting sprint racing. It's called the Action Track, and there's a reason for that.

In one 1955 race Duane Carter, Sr., charged for the finish line with Ed Elisian and Johnny Boyd, all in a group. Could he have imagined that twenty years later, almost to the month, his son, then four years old and watching from the grandstands, would be doing the same thing in an almost identical car?

Sprint cars have changed very little in size and shape over the years, and they have remained dangerous. They are designed and built very carefully to do one thing—to get around a dirt-surfaced oval track as quickly as possible—and they do that better than anything else.

Sprint cars are still the proving ground for young drivers on the way up.

In 1975 Duane Carter, Jr., lined up for the annual Tony Hulman Classic at the Terre Haute track, the hotbed of sprint car racing in the Midwest. The name of the race was new that year, but it was a continuation of a traditional series of races dating back to Carter, Sr. But this time it was Senior in the pits and Junior on the track, exactly the way they both wanted it.

Duane Carter, Sr., adjusts the fire-retarding skirt on the helmet of his champion son, Duane Carter, Jr. *(Bart Hagerman, Valvoline Oil)*

Alongside Pancho Carter in the front row was defending sprint car champion Gary Bettenhausen. All young up-and-coming drivers in the business, along with some veterans, were there in the field when Tony Hulman, owner of the Indianapolis Speedway, took the microphone for the start of the exciting race.

"Gentlemen, start your engines!" shouted Tony Hulman. Push trucks moved forward. The race named in his honor was under way.

The first turn of a sprint car race on a dirt track, just after the green flag falls, is an unbelievable mixture of sound, smells, and action. The entire field of cars, often very evenly matched, charging from the start, rushes toward the first turn. Dirt tracks are small, not wide and long like Indy or Ontario. The field has to funnel into the turn, with everybody accelerating, everybody anxious to move up, everybody throwing dirt from digging rear wheels, everybody seemingly lost in a sea of engine noise and caroming race cars, everybody wanting to be in the same place at the same time—the lead. On the first lap or so action is sometimes unbelievable. The tension is nerve-racking.

Carter, Bettenhausen, and others made it through the turns on that bright Sunday afternoon, but behind them trouble developed. On the backstretch of the first lap the wheels of Jim McElreath's sprinter touched the wheels of Chuck Booth's car, and both cars ricocheted apart. Booth spun to a harmless stop, but McElreath flipped end over end three times and crashed on top of the retaining wall. Then he bounced over into a parking lot. The veteran driver was seriously injured. One of the first to aid the luckless McElreath was Chuck Booth, who leaped from his own racer and worked to extract McElreath from his overturned car before the rescue workers arrived.

Carter raced on, with Bettenhausen inches behind. The remainder of the field snarled in a pack a few feet behind Bettenhausen.

As Duane Carter, Sr., watched his son battle to hold the lead, he remembered holding the same jerking wheel himself, fighting for control of the same bouncing car, stoically accepted the same danger as his son. If anybody outside the race knew how hard young Carter was working at that moment, it had to be the elder Carter.

Duane Carter, Jr., is good—better, in the opinion of many fans who have seen them both, than his father. He held on in the exciting race, but behind him by only a car length was the persistent Bettenhausen. Behind Bettenhausen battled six more cars. At every turn the positions changed behind Carter and Bettenhausen. Finally, in a desperate gamble to pass the speeding Carter near the end of the race, Gary Bettenhausen skidded high: he tapped the wall, and dropped far back in the field.

Duane Carter, Sr., stood in the pits smiling, knowing how the young driver on the track felt at that moment. Duane Carter, Jr., took the checkered flag for the most important victory of his career to that point.

Young Carter's racing style is different from his

father's, though "both are excellent drivers," according to racing expert Jim Lunt of the *National Speed Sport News*. "Duane, Sr., was more cautious and proven in every division in which he raced. Pancho is more daring and he is still learning, especially at Indianapolis."

"I've wanted to drive at Indianapolis since I was six weeks old," says Pancho Carter. "That's when I came to the Speedway for the first time when Dad was running tire tests." In 1974 he had not yet been in an Indy-type car, that tricky mechanical marvel made to turn left and go very fast. But driving at Indy is more than simply stepping on the gas and steering the car around the old oval: each turn is different, and cars have many different adjustments, each one critical. Modern cars have turbochargers that boost the power of the engine by using the exhaust gas pressure. Drivers must be aware of such hazards as the booster kicking in because of too much pressure on the gas pedal while they are in a lower gear. This action can kick the rear wheels so hard that the rear end of the car lifts off the track. There are many such problems with driving an exceptionally high-performance car, problems which often rule out a first-year driver's attempt to pass his qualification test.

Carter practiced for only two weeks and then took his driver's test, a ten-lap, four-phase drive at fixed speeds. In this test, officials, other drivers, and observers stationed around the track report on the smoothness and skill of the one being tested.

Unlike dozens of other young drivers trying Indy for

Duane Carter, Jr., on the line for the 1975 Indy race. This is the car
he wrecked only days before. *(Author)*

the first time, Carter, like his father years before, was flawless. After the race that year he was awarded the Rookie of the Year award for being the best all-around new driver in the field. He finished in seventh place and won $28,000 for his day's work.

In the 1975 Indy race he signed on with Dan Gurney's team of All-American Racers, perhaps the luckiest break of his career.

Gurney's Eagles, Indy-type championship cars, had won just about everything. They were the racers to beat, the car many other race drivers bought to drive themselves. In one Indy 500 more than half the cars were Eagles built by Dan Gurney. The Eagle "factory" job was open with the departure of champion Bobby Unser, a two-time Indy winner. Duane Carter, Jr., got the call. But despite this break, in 1975 he had problems that no other driver in history has had.

The 1975 Indianapolis 500 was held on May 25. The final qualifying session had been on May 18. By the evening of the 18th the final gun had sounded, and it was all over. Quiet settled over the speedway. The stands emptied and clean-up crews began getting the giant plant ready for race day. With no race cars roaring past, workmen took the chance to patch and groom the track.

Race cars that had qualified for the race were being polished and painted afresh and tuned and decaled with new sponsors' names. Cars of drivers who hadn't made it were loaded onto trailers and into trucks for the long, sad ride home.

The field was set, and Duane Carter, Jr., was in. He had qualified at a respectable 183 miles per hour for the outside spot in the sixth row. The fastest car in the field was A. J. Foyt's Gilmore Special, which had qualified at 194 miles per hour. The slowest car, driven by Californian Mike Hiss, was recorded at 181 miles per hour.

Carter was certain his Cobra Tire "Special" had a chance at finishing up front.

From the final gun at qualifying to the start of the race, no cars are allowed on the track, except for a quick three-hour period. These three hours are allowed a day or so before race day for "final carburetion tuning." The term is an anachronism dating from when race cars actually had carburetors. In modern racing fuel injection is common, so the three hours are used for last-minute adjustments to the chassis and engine.

With minutes remaining in the final carburetion period, Carter decided to "crank it on" for one last quick lap to check out a new chassis setup. Coming through turn one he nicked the apex, spun, rocketed to the outside, smashed the wall tailfirst, shot back down across the track and nearly destroyed his car in a nose dive into a drainage ditch. Stunned and in agony from torn back muscles and other injuries, Carter crawled from the wreckage. He looked at what was left of the racer. He'd really done a good job on it. It was a mess.

Could his dream have ended on carburetion day? Nobody had ever crashed out of the famous 500 in such a way. He couldn't believe his luck.

Carter's 1975 racer moved to the garages as mechanics, who thought their work was done until race day, worked desperately to put the smashed car back together. There was no rule at Indy to cover a qualified car that had been wrecked. There was no more chance for Carter to qualify in another one. For Duane Carter at that race, it was that car, wrecked as it was, or no car.

Hours before the race was to start the repairs were completed. By that time hundreds of high-school band musicians celebrating race day were swarming over the track. With no chance for a track test the car was an unknown quantity as it was pushed to the line.

Would Carter's racer even start? Would the suspension hold up through welds and jury-rigged parts? The frame? The tub? Would the chassis setup work for high-speed racing? Was the steering correct?

"Gentlemen, start your engines!"

Thirty-two engines roared to life, then thirty-three, as Carter's engine caught and thundered. Slowly the field pulled away behind the speeding pace car and aligned itself for the start.

Bobby Unser, the 1968 Indy winner, won the 1975 race in a blinding rain storm, with racers slipping and sliding and fans running for shelter. It was one of those midwestern gully-washers that sneak up and then cut loose with torrents.

In second place was a happy Johnny Rutherford, the 1974 winner, and in third place was three-time winner A. J. Foyt. Many said, and Foyt agreed, that if the rain had not come he would have won. His strategy had been to lie in wait in third place until near the end. He was just beginning to make his move when the race was stopped prematurely.

Three former winners, an incredibly experienced trio of racing champions, had placed first-second-third. Still battling for the lead at the end, with a car he was holding together by sheer force of will, was Duane Carter, Jr. In the car that had been almost completely destroyed after qualifying, he finished fourth. He finished ahead of Indy veterans like Roger McCluskey, Al Unser, and Mario Andretti.

In the pits Duane Carter, Sr., smiled. He had once finished fourth in the same big race. He knew how great his son was feeling.

Mickey's mother was a nurse and she agreed. The parents conferred, and the father announced the decision: there would be no amputation. When the doctors protested that Mickey might die, Mickey's father firmly explained his position. He felt that the original doctor had pinched an artery and that rebreaking and resetting the arm would correct the situation, even if the X-rays didn't show it that way. Mickey waited.

"Mr. Thompson," asked the doctor gently, "do you want to save the arm or save the boy?"

Thompson looked at his son, his pride and joy. Mickey was strong already. He was tough. His future was good. With only one arm his life might be ruined. "If you put it that bluntly, doctor, I guess I'm going to be pretty blunt too. If I bury the arm I'm going to bury the boy along with it. There will be no amputation at this time."

"We'll give it one last try," the doctor agreed.

So the two men took the young boy's arm. The doctor braced while the father pulled the break apart and then worked the arm around. Both men finally agreed that if the artery had been pinched, it was pinched no longer. The arm was reset, and soon evidence of new circulation appeared. The arm had been saved.

"It wasn't a pleasant experience for me," Mickey Thompson recalls, "but Dad says I never whimpered. That was the way he trained me."

Mickey Thompson loved cars. When he was eleven years old, he took money he had been saving and bought an old jalopy for seven dollars. This was okay with his father, since Mickey had earned the money delivering papers, mowing lawns, and helping neighborhood garage mechanics. There was just one problem: he was too young to drive. He had no license. In this case, though, it didn't matter because the car wouldn't run. Among other matters the pistons were rusted solid in the cylinders.

Even at that age Mickey Thompson had spirit and inventiveness. He tore the rusting hulk into pieces, hauled them home one at a time in a little wagon, then reassembled them in the family garage.

The car ran perfectly when he was finished.

So he sold it for $125.

When Mickey Thompson grew up, he worked for a time as a pressman for the Los Angeles *Times,* but his real interest remained cars. He kept building them, and he began to race them also. He started a family and had a son, Dannie.

By the time Dannie was nine Mickey was devoting his energy mainly to drag racing in his custom-built cars. Dannie had acquired an interest in the sport too; while the father drove at the drag strip the son competed next door in quarter-midget races. Mickey Thompson had made a name for himself as one of the best designers and builders of custom race cars around, and the little racer he had rigged up for Dannie put the boy in good shape for the competitions. Dannie was off to a good start on what was to be his own life's occupation.

But one night a near-disaster altered the course of

the racing future for both Thompsons. At the midget races a young driver attempted to pass, but skidded wide and flipped into the air. The little racer bounced twice and landed upside down and smoking on the wall. Track workers, mostly parents of the drivers, rushed to the scene.

In the confusion a spectator who was mistaken both about the driver and the extent of his injuries ran to the neighboring drag strip to tell Mickey Thompson, "Dannie has broken his back!"

Mickey's face went white. He had seen many crashes, and his own body carried the scars of many accidents. But now in a flash, he saw auto racing as nothing but horror. As he ran full speed toward the midget track, fear for his son was overcome by remorse that he had encouraged him, even built his car.

But then he saw Dannie, alive and well, standing in the pits. And the other youngster was bruised, but not so much that he wouldn't stay on for the rest of the race. Still, Mickey's mind had been made up by the close call. There would be no more race driving for Dannie Thompson.

Nor was there, for many years.

But Dannie still wanted to race. At seventeen, after finishing high school, he quietly obtained a motorcycle. Evenings, without being specific about where he was going, he would head for the race track. He won the very first race he entered, also the second, the third, and the fourth. He was a natural race driver, at least on motorcycles.

Then one day a call came home from Mickey, who

Dannie Thompson ready for an off-road race in a single-seater. (*Ross D. Olney photo*)

was away on business. He spoke quietly, as though fearful of the answer he would get.

"Dannie, are you racing motorcycles?" The bike magazines had been praising the skill of the young rider and one issue had come across his father's desk.

"Yes," answered Dannie.

So Mickey came to watch. "The first time my father came to see me race, it was motorcycles," Dannie recalls. To his dismay, I won the first two races, and then while leading the third, I had a very bad crash. I think it was then that I realized he was afraid I was going to get hurt."

Mickey Thompson made another decision, and a driving team was formed soon after that now is favored wherever it races. On the side of its magnificently crafted racers designed for off-road racing appear the words "Co-drivers, Mickey Thompson, Dannie Thompson."

Mickey Thompson has lost some races, of course, and he has had many other disappointments. But his sheer determination, his perseverance, and his perfectionism have thrust him to great victories. This character is shared by the son, who is willing to expend everything in an effort to win, regardless of personal discomfort or danger.

Dannie remembers one of his father's greatest victories, which began rather laughably after a long effort. The problem was that any program of racing must be planned to the last detail to be successful, and whatever the effort, it must be financed from a bottomless purse. Racing is very expensive. For a hot-rod pressman at the Los Angeles *Times* to decide to become the fastest man on wheels was . . . well . . . a little comical. Mickey Thompson had built a certain record on the salt flats, but he had no money, no backing, and questionable design talent. Who did he think he was?

Those who had whispered before laughed out loud when Thompson began to build his world speed record car from cast-offs and junk parts.

Junk parts! Mickey Thompson actually raided the trash bins outside Los Angeles auto dealers for parts thrown away by mechanics. And these were stock parts at that, not carefully designed or critically machined. Yet he planned to use them in a racer he would drive faster than anything had ever been driven before.

As word leaked out, people came to see the strange Mickey Thompson machine. Was he building a single powerful super-engine? No. Thompson felt that if one engine would go fast, four would go four times as fast. He was building his car, named *Challenger,* with four engines. That meant four transmissions and four of everything else with astonishingly critical coordination necessary between it all. The driver, Thompson himself, was going to sit in a cockpit slung out behind the rear axle.

"He'll wipe himself out in a blaze of mechanical stupidity," insisted one critic.

Paying no attention, Thompson rebuilt four junked

Pontiac engines. He scrimped and saved and built. Finally Goodyear began to believe him and agreed to provide special tires for the high-speed run. Thompson doubled his hours at the *Times* as the need for money increased. His wife worked. He borrowed and mortgaged. His retired father worked. Gradually other sponsors came in with small amounts of money, and the racer took shape.

Finally the thirty-two separate fuel injectors began to work together, the four engines—two forward and two set backward, running in reverse—blended into an idle without shaking the frame apart. The transmissions, through a series of Thompson-designed linkages, shifted at the same time.

But on its first outing the car was a disaster. It skidded out of control and tore its own gear boxes apart. It refused to perform at all as Thompson had promised. Critics nodded sagely as the car and its disappointed crew went back home to Long Beach, California.

For two more years this man who never quits worked on the car, spending night after lonely night in the garage, solving problem after problem. Then, on September 9, 1960, he thundered to an incredible 406.6 miles per hour on the salt flats, the fastest speed ever attained by an engine-driven car.

As he had promised, Mickey Thompson had become the fastest man on earth.

Most fans of off-road racing know that the sport punishes both car and driver, but few have any real idea of the incredible pain and strain to be endured. It would take the opportunity to strap in and ride on an off-road course with a driver like either of the Thompsons to understand for certain.

The seats of the cars are designed with the care of space-capsule seats. They are formed to fit the individual driver's body. The driver is strapped in with a suspension system that has been heavily padded with foam and fur. During the run, the straps are tightened to the point of pain—the slightest amount of give would almost certainly mean torn muscles and, possibly, some snapped bones. The driver and co-driver in a two-seater become a part of the seat, and the seat is a part of the frame of the racer.

Handholds are welded in place for the co-driver so that his arms don't flop around dangerously, and leg braces are installed for both men to help steady them in their seats.

When an off-road race car bounces past spectators, they can see the jerking of the machine and the snapping of the driver's head and body. What doesn't show is the terrible muscular effort needed to hold the head and body in place and to keep the internal organs from injury through jolting. It is not the same as an acrobat throwing his body through controlled movements with the muscles cushioning as well as propelling. This is a situation where muscles must hold firm against great centrifugal and lateral forces.

Off-road racers fly off ridges and slam violently against rock-hard ground. Everything seems off-

Off-road racing is rugged! Here, Mickey and Dannie Thompson's truck bounds over a lump in the track. It will hit *hard*. *(Ross D. Olney photo)*

camber and pulls unnaturally in unusual directions. The pain for the driver is often intense.

One reporter rode with drivers over an average off-road course, not the easiest course on the circuit, but far from the most difficult. After a couple of laps he was helped from the car white-faced from pain, not believing that man and machine could survive such sustained treatment over an entire race. It seemed days before his insides were back in place.

Mickey Thompson has received many injuries from this kind of racing. He has even broken his back. For this reason Dannie now drives the roughest parts of courses. Both seem to thrive on the extreme experience of off-road racing, and both thrive on each other's company.

Perhaps it is true that those who live fastest and hardest live the best.

Of course, Mickey Thompson can get anybody he wants to drive his great cars. He has had on his team as driver men like Duane Carter, Sr., World Champion Graham Hill, and Dan Gurney.

Thompson could have gently praised his son and put him to work in the pits. Perhaps he felt like doing just that, for he has some unhappy memories. But Mickey Thompson didn't do that. He picked his son to drive not for who he is, but for what he is, a race driver of promise. Mickey Thompson sees much of himself in his son. He recognizes in the young lion his own unquenchable enthusiasm and desire to win.

Dannie Thompson muscles his single-seat off-road racer around a bumpy curve at Riverside Raceway. *(Ross D. Olney photo)*

Being the son of a famous racing father has helped, though Dannie raced on his own for some time before joining his father. But there have been drawbacks for the young driver.

"When you have a father like mine and you are trying to get sponsorship help on your own for your own effort, they always say, 'Well, your father has money, why not go to him?'

"Now we are driving together. I even designed and built a shock-absorbing seat for his back. It pivots and has shocks to help absorb the rough ride."

Sounds like something Mickey would have done.

Co-driving the world's major races with off-road king Mickey Thompson is not an easy assignment. It's glamorous, exciting, and rewarding, but there's much more to it than that.

Dannie Thompson reports to the shop for work at five in the morning. They count it an early evening, with time to do something else, if the boss closes down for the night before 10 P.M. Preparing a racer for an upcoming off-road race sometimes means building a brand-new car. It's a full-time job and then some.

"Sure I have a girl friend," Dannie says with a grin. "But she sometimes forgets what I look like when we are getting ready for a race."

Mickey Thompson is a dedicated man, driven by an inner urge to be the very best at what he is doing. This drive has carried over to his son.

"I'm hoping off-road racing is just a starter for me," Dannie explains. "Formula 5000 intrigues me. Formula

1 intrigues me. I've even talked to my dad about
Formula 5000, but he is negative so far."

As the years pass and the son continues to mature, it
will be interesting to see if he will develop the way his
father has. Mickey Thompson grew up in a tough
neighborhood, and he has a violent temper. Yet he can
be moved to tears on many occasions. His values are
motherhood-and-apple-pie old-fashioned. He will
glare angrily at users of profanity. He pays attention to
remembering names, paying debts, and responding to
kindnesses, and he believes that hard work and
perseverance will be rewarded, while laziness will not.
He's willing to fight for his traditional values.

But sometimes in quiet moments, his gaze drifts off.
He doesn't hear, if spoken to, and his smile is vacant.
Perhaps he is remembering the day at the drag strip
when he thought his son had crashed, or the day in
Mexico when he crashed into five bystanders.

He never dwells on his great victories and that adds
to his character. But he seems to remember the great
defeats, and that adds, too.

Dannie Thompson could do much worse than mature
alongside his father.

5 BETTENHAUSEN

There was probably not a driver on the track during the 1971 Indy 500 who had a deeper desire to win than Gary Bettenhausen. He was from a racing family, his father had been a great racing driver, and both his younger brothers were race drivers. But no Bettenhausen had ever won the big race, the Indy 500. The senior Bettenhausen had raced at Indy fourteen times without a victory. Both the younger brothers were standing by to race there as their experience grew. Gary himself had raced in that famous race three times before without a victory.

Bettenhausen, a handsome young driver, can be reluctant to talk about his profession, but he gladly discusses the "destiny" of some Bettenhausen eventually to win an Indy race.

The Bettenhausens have been plagued by bad luck, but their own humanity has interfered with their Indy efforts, too.

Cruising down the backstretch during the 1971 race,

Gary Bettenhausen (left) with his pal Bill Vukovich before an Indianapolis Speedway race. *(Indianapolis Speedway photo)*

Gary Bettenhausen once again felt that this could be the year when, at long last, a Bettenhausen could swing his racer into Victory Lane at the old Speedway. Watching the race were his mother, his two racing brothers, and a sister. The highest moment of the family would be when a Bettenhausen won that race.

The race continued. Up ahead, out of Gary's vision, Mike Mosley whipped out of control coming out of the fourth turn. His Murphy Stores Special slammed violently into the retaining wall and the body buckled, pinning the driver inside. Then the car shot off the wall and across the track, narrowly missing several other cars. Finally it crashed into two other racers which had been wrecked before and were parked off the track along the inside wall. Flames shot up from the wreckage.

Mosley, seriously injured, was still trapped in his cockpit.

Gary Bettenhausen was roaring down the short straightaway between turns three and four. Ahead, other racers were swerving to avoid the Mosley crash. Bettenhausen guided his car down and into the fourth turn, still chasing his family dream. Then he saw the wreckage ahead. He realized instantly that Mosley was trapped in his car and that race traffic was preventing safety crewmen and firemen from reaching the scene. Only seconds had passed since the crash.

Winning the Indy 500 is one thing, but on a higher level there is helping an injured fellow driver whose life is in grave danger. Gary Bettenhausen hit his brakes and swerved his racer. Stopping, unbuckling, grabbing a fire extinguisher from a safety apron, he ran to the scene. He battled the flames and held them at bay until rescue squads arrived to finish the job and cut Mosley from the wreckage. Only then did Bettenhausen reenter the race. He had been the only driver to stop. He finished in tenth place.

Mosley lived to race again, and Bettenhausen raced on, chasing the family dream, helping his brothers to do the same, and always wanting more than anything else to beat the old track that took his father when he was a boy.

For seven years, from 1961 through 1968, the name Bettenhausen, a name that brought visions of racing excitement to every fan, did not ring out at Indy.

In 1961 Tony Bettenhausen, father of three racing sons, was preparing for his fifteenth Indy 500.

Tony Bettenhausen was a fixture in motor racing. Twice National Driving Champion (in 1951 and again in 1953, even though some claimed he was past his prime) and a skilled competitor in all types of racers, Tony Bettenhausen was known as a hard charger. Although he had never won the famous five-hundred-mile race, several times he had placed high in the final standings.

It was typical of the friendly Bettenhausen on that cool, clear, fast practice day that he volunteered to test a pal's car for him. Paul Russo had been having problems handling his beautiful red-and-gold-leaf Watson roadster, the same car Rodger Ward had won

Tony Bettenhausen shakes hands with driver Bill Cheesbourg before the start of the 1957 race. Bettenhausen drove one of the famous Novi racers in this event. *(Author)*

with in 1959. Setting up a race car is a matter of practice, mechanical knowledge, seat-of-the-pants feel, and patience. Some drivers can go out for a few laps and then instruct mechanics just what to do to make the car feel smooth and hard on the track instead of bouncy and loose.

Bettenhausen was one of the most skilled at setting up. It was no big deal to him to help a competitor. He was glad to do it. Russo's car had been handling poorly and was not really safe to drive, but Tony was willing.

It was mid-afternoon when he pulled Russo's sparkling number 24 out of the pits. Only one other car was practicing on the track at that time, though more than fifty racers had been warming up during the morning practice period. Young Lloyd Ruby, the solitary driver, was on the backstretch as Bettenhausen came out of number four turn at speed.

Momentarily he seemed to slow down, as if to pull into the pit entrance. Then apparently changing his mind, he decided to take another lap. He increased speed down the straightaway and flashed over the starting line. Suddenly, without warning, the car veered to the left and climbed the low retaining wall.

It flipped several times along the top of the wall, rolling itself into a cocoon of wire safety fencing. It tore the fence's steel posts from their concrete mounts and tossed them like so many straws in the wind. Horrified observers watched the clouds of smoke and dust that boiled up and the dull red glow that appeared as the wreckage burst into flames.

Safety men and firemen rushed to the crash, but it was already too late for the Flying Dutchman. The seemingly indestructible farmer from Tinley Park, Illinois, had survived many crashes during his great career, but not this one.

He left three sons, Gary, Merle, and Tony Lee.

Tony Lee Bettenhausen, youngest of the three racing brothers, best remembers his father leading the five-hundred-mile race at Indianapolis in 1958, one of his most exciting feats. "I think he would have helped me if I chose to race," says young Tony, "but he wouldn't have pushed me into it."

Race fans have said that regardless of Gary's obvious skill or middle brother Merle's on-again, off-again racing career, it could be that young Tony has the best shot of all at the big race. Rather than the open-wheel, open-cockpit cars of his brothers, Tony chose the stock car route. In 1972 he was second in NASCAR National Late Model Sportsmen points. In a kind of racing that attracts the biggest names in the sport, men with years of experience in Grand National racing, Tony was second overall.

Racing talent runs in the Bettenhausen family, but racing luck does not. In 1972 Merle Bettenhausen, the always smiling middle brother who seemed a natural for racing, finally got his chance at the "big cars," the Indy-type racers his older brother had been driving, the kind of racers in which their father had achieved his greatest fame.

Championship cars, they are called, and they race on

Tony Lee Bettenhausen straps in for a NASCAR race at Riverside International Raceway in California. *(Author)*

a circuit called the Championship Trail. It includes Indianapolis as well as such high-speed paved tracks as Ontario Motor Speedway, Pocono International Speedway, and the fast paved tracks at Phoenix, Trenton, and Milwaukee. Doing the Trail is a year's racing for this type of racer. At the end of the year a National Driving Champion is selected on the basis of his season's performance.

The banked speedway at Brooklyn, Michigan, is also on the Championship Trail. It was at this fast track, known as Michigan International Speedway, that Merle Bettenhausen got his first chance at the big cars. The disastrous outcome was witnessed by millions on national television.

The famous Jim Hurtubise was a close witness to Merle Bettenhausen's accident. "Merle was high and started fishtailing," said Hurtubise. "I backed off because I didn't know where he was going. Suddenly he went into the outer rail with the right front and the car seemed to explode."

Television confirmed Hurtubise's report. The Bettenhausen racer lurched hard into the outside wall, slid along it, and slammed the wall again very hard. Almost immediately it burst into flames. The Kingfish Offy had hit the steel guard rail and driven partially under it, shearing away the right side of the car. The turbocharger, a power-boosting device on the engine, was ripped free and thrown onto grass far outside the track, where it started a fire with its heat. Then the car, entirely lacking its right side, wheels and all, skidded

Merle Bettenhausen, the middle brother, in the cockpit of an Indy-type car before his accident. (*Bart Hagerman, Valvoline Oil*)

on down the backstretch for thirty-three yards. All the while the driver was fighting to get out before the car stopped in flames.

Prompt track fire trucks chased the sliding car down the track, and one fireman jumped into the car and battled to help the driver escape. Both men were seriously burned.

Merle Bettenhausen remained conscious throughout and tried to help his rescuer. But he could not lift himself up from the broken, burning racer.

Later he recalled the accident to Chris Economaki, editor of *National Speed Sport News:* "It exploded when it hit, so right away I unhooked and started to get out. Then the car hit the rail a second time and threw me into it.

"There went the arm," he finished.

Bettenhausen was not immediately aware that he had actually lost his right arm, so he could not understand why he was having such trouble hoisting himself from the cockpit. To him it felt as though he were still strapped in.

The close knit Bettenhausens care for each other and they have a love for motor racing that is difficult for outsiders to comprehend. For three days the middle brother was in critical condition with burns and loss of blood. On the third day, from his hospital bed Merle Bettenhausen smiled the broad, open grin he was famous for. Though still listed in serious condition, he spoke with strong confidence.

"I'll be back next year," he said cheerfully. "My

brother Gary is out now lining up power steering units for a midget and a stock car." His enthusiasm was evident.

The flaming 190-mile-per-hour crash had been a setback, but nothing more. With the help of power steering Merle would drive again. His brother would take care of things while he recovered so all would be ready when he was.

Merle Bettenhausen did drive again, and he won some races, but in the end he retired. He walked away after he had successfully come back, though, and that was important.

"One of us will win Indy some day," says Gary Bettenhausen. "It has got to be. We feel that our dad handed down a legacy to us and that a Bettenhausen is destined to win. If, for some reason, I don't make it, then Merle will get a chance. And if he doesn't, then there's always Tony Lee. We believe it's our destiny."

Gary Bettenhausen crashed at Indianapolis in 1968, and he had engine trouble in 1969 and 1970. In 1971 he stopped to help Mike Mosley. In 1972, driving the sleek Penske McClaren Offenhauser and leading with only twenty-five laps to go, he had engine trouble.

In 1973, a sad year of fire and death at Indy, Bettenhausen came close, placing fifth in his Sunoco McClaren. It was a disaster in 1974—he finished thirty-second in a field of thirty-three. In 1975 he was running a fine race when on lap 158 a suspension member suddenly snapped and he crashed, sliding and

In the 1975 Indy race Gary Bettenhausen lost a wheel and crashed and scraped all the way down the main stretch, throwing sparks out behind. (*Author*)

bouncing his three-wheeled car all the way down the main stretch.

Still, Gary Bettenhausen is considered one of the top young lions in the sport of auto racing. In sprint car driving, one of the toughest divisions of the sport, he has been National Champion more than once. He is a superb midget race car driver. At Indianapolis and at other national championship events he is smooth and consistent. He is a member of the inner circle of auto racing, as was his father.

Of course the Bettenhausen name has helped. "The name was recognized and admired. It opened doors and got me in to see the right people," says Gary. But the name could also be a hindrance. "People expected too much from a beginner. They were too quick to criticize."

There is a Championship Trail race track at College Station, Texas, called the Texas World Speedway. Gary Bettenhausen qualified in the well-prepared Penske Sunoco Offy for the October 1973 race there. Although gridded well back in the field in fourteenth place, behind such drivers as Mario Andretti, Gordon Johncock, A. J. Foyt, and Al Unser, fans acknowledged that Bettenhausen had, as always, a good chance to win.

In this race, though, it developed that Johnny Rutherford was on top. He was leading in the latter stages of the contest, and his car seemed as though it would run on forever just a shade faster than the second-place car close behind.

That was the magnificent blue-and-yellow car of Gary Bettenhausen. He had worked his way up through the field, and everybody in the grandstands was already awarding him the substantial purse for runner-up. Almost lying down in the cockpit, strapped in, his fire suit and full-face helmet giving him the appearance of a spaceman, Bettenhausen planned his strategy. He realized that with just a little more pressure on the gas pedal he might pass the fast-running Rutherford before the end. He decided to give it the old Bettenhausen try. His father would have done the same.

With ten laps to go he said to his pit crew over his two-way radio, "I can pass him. I'm going after him." The pit crew had to understand exactly what was happening, for both the front-running cars would need one more quick stop for fuel. The battle on the track continued with Gary Bettenhausen glued to the oil-blackened rear of Rutherford's car.

Then the call came over the radio: "Rush in for fuel. Give up the chase and stop for gas, or you might not make it to the end."

Quickly Bettenhausen steered his racer down pit row, where men swarmed over it the instant he stopped. He rejected a quick drink of water offered by one crewman at the end of a long stick. Meanwhile a measured amount of fuel was dumped in—not a full tank, but just enough to allow him to finish. After only twelve seconds he roared back onto the track.

Fans were on their feet cheering as, just then,

Rutherford streaked into his pit for fuel. At that moment Bettenhausen was whining on down the backstretch.

It took seventeen seconds for Rutherford to fuel up. When he rushed back into the race, the two cars were still nose-to-tail. But this time it was Gary Bettenhausen in the lead.

Despite two yellow flag incidents in the last eight laps which slowed the field and allowed Rutherford to jump ahead as the green flag was waved, Bettenhausen held the lead he had battled for. This time when the checkered flag dropped it was Gary Bettenhausen, in the blue Penske McClaren, waving at the crowd.

6 PARSONS

In the big picture the late-season race at DuQouin Speedway in Illinois in 1948 was not all that significant. The National Driving Championship had already been decided. In fact, the champion was in the field that day and so were many other top drivers of the moment. This was a Championship Trail race, but the stands were far from full. The day was icy, the sunshine was cold and thin, and a blustery wind promised worse weather yet.

Qualifications had been delayed for one thing and then another. Officials seemed reluctant to hurry matters along, and fans were losing interest. Not the most exciting of days at DuQuoin Speedway, but for two drivers in the race, it was to be critical.

One was Ted Horn, the National Driving Champion. Ted didn't have to be there at all. He had already won the championship and he did not need the money. He merely felt he owed something to the fans and the race promoters. More spectators would come if the champion was in the race, and the purse and the profit would

Johnnie Parsons (left), former National Driving Champion and 1950 Indy winner, and his son Johnny, now a championship car driver. (*Bart Hagerman, Valvoline Oil*)

therefore be larger. Horn was racing for one of his favorite children's charity groups just to make the day worthwhile.

The other driver who would find this day one of the most important in his life was a young charger who was driving one of his first championship races. Nobody knew then how far he might go in racing; they barely knew who he was. He was tall, handsome, and immaculately turned out with a shining car and a fine driving uniform. He had turned from show business, where his parents were well known, to become a racing driver.

Eventually he would reach the top of the sport and be where the great Horn was on that day. But in 1948 young Johnny Parsons was a beginner racing against the big names. He was at the bottom of one of the toughest ladders in sports.

Another thing stands out about this long-ago race. From that day on all parts of all racing cars in sanctioned events were required to be "magnafluxed"—X-rayed— to pinpoint any internal flaws that might cause a failure under the strain of racing. For a flawed part caused a crash that day, and a driver died.

The race steward finally crawled into the idling pace car and pulled onto the track before the grid of cars. One by one the racers fell in behind, running cold, stuttering and smoking at the low speed. Gradually the fans emerged from blankets and overcoats to watch the action, but, perhaps because of the weather, spirits still seemed damp at the track. Fans stayed quiet, the pits were subdued, and even photographers did not seem anxious to begin shooting.

The field roared out of the fourth turn on the old dirt track and bunched for the start. In the pack Johnnie Parsons was thrilled beyond measure. Here he was, driving wheel to wheel with the likes of Ted Horn, Rex Mays, Myron Fohr, Mel Hanson, and Paul Russo. He was confident, but also keenly aware of how long he had waited and of how many little races it had taken to be where he was then.

The field of snarling racers battled together into the first turn in a great cloud of dust and dirt from the hard-packed track. Up front was Ted Horn, trying to move past pole-position holder Rex Mays.

Increasing speed, they rushed through the second turn and down the backstretch. Gradually they began to string out as they snarled through the third turn, the fourth turn, and back onto the main stretch.

Now strung into a closely packed nose-to-tail row, they slammed once again into the first turn. Suddenly a huge cloud of dust and dirt flew up, obscuring the cars. Up and into the clear for an instant came a white car with a blue tail. On the tail was the gold number 1, the number of the champion. This car dropped back into the dust cloud. Almost instantly another car, a blue one, shot up, only to drop back again out of sight.

The field was much slower as it left the cloud. Officials rushed to the scene and discovered that the blue car, belonging to Johnny Mantz, was wrecked. Mantz was injured.

Meanwhile Rex Mays left the slowly circling field, now held back by a caution flag. Grimly Mays drove his car to the pits, to his trailer, and prepared to leave. He had been in the dust cloud, and he had seen what happened.

The blue-and-white car with the number 1 did not seem that badly damaged. The front wheels had come off, probably because of a failed wheel spindle. But the driver lay crumpled on the edge of the track near the car, and that was what Mays had seen. He knew that champion Ted Horn was dead.

Racing men race, however, and soon this race was resumed, though the racers drove with heavy hearts. At the end a new winner was crowned. Young Johnnie Parsons, a driver who eventually outdrove them all and went on to win both a National Driving Championship and the Indy 500, had won his very first championship race.

On the sidelines were his wife and three-year-old son Johnny who cheered even if he didn't understand. Planted in the little boy was a spark which would grow into a love for the noise, excitement, and thrill of auto racing.

The father, Johnnie with an *ie,* is known to many as Gentleman Johnnie. He is one of racing's most excellent representatives ever. He always had the neatest crew, the cleanest car, and the most immaculate uniform. He was one of the best spokesmen for racing, doing much to lift the sport from greasy T-shirts to the modern age of shine and precision.

Auto Racing's Young Lions

Gentleman Johnnie spoke eloquently on many subjects besides auto racing. He was at home around racing men because he was a superb driver, but he was as different from most of them as day from night. He stood out in a crowd. His eyes snapped and his smile was contagious. He was the picture of a racing champion.

Because of his show business background, many entertainment stars were his pals. Clark Gable frequented his pit as did many other motion picture personalities.

At the drivers' meeting the day before the 1950 Indianapolis race, the weather report was for rain. Everybody laughed. It wouldn't dare rain on an Indy race! (It seldom did until recently.) Even if it was raining early in the morning, by race time it was always clear, dry, and warm—and fast.

"But I got thinking about it," said Johnnie Parsons. "Back in the garage I told my crew, 'Boys, the weatherman has never been wrong yet. He has never predicted rain before, but now he does. I think we should pay attention and go all out right at the start to collect all the lap money we can get.' " (They pay $200 to the leader of each lap in a five-hundred mile race, so that, theoretically, a driver leading all two hundred laps could earn an extra $40,000. This has never happened.)

The next day, just before the race was to get under way, Parsons still thought his plan was best. He would

Three all-time-great race drivers and representatives of the sport, Wilbur Shaw (left), Johnnie Parsons (center), and Ralph DePalma, who once pushed his car over the line at Indy. *(Indianapolis Speedway photo)*

run as hard as he could, get into the lead, then hope that his car would hold together. If it rained, he would still be up front.

Then came a bombshell.

"We've got a real problem, Johnnie," said his chief mechanic.

"What's wrong?" asked the driver, all suited up and ready to race.

"The engine has a cracked block!" the mechanic replied. A cracked block, a crack in the side of the engine. An engine like that wouldn't last long in a passenger car on the street, let alone during the five hundred grueling miles of one of the toughest races in the world.

By then it was too late to change engines. There was nothing anybody could do. Parsons considered the problem and made his decision. He would still go as hard and fast as he could, collecting what lap money he could until it rained—or until the engine blew apart.

True to his plan, Johnnie Parsons drove his Wynn's Friction Proofing "Special" into the lead early in the race. Lap after lap he fought off drivers like Mauri Rose, who ran at him again and again attempting to take the lead. The engine in Parsons' car continued to sing.

Overhead, black clouds began to build up. Fans watched both the hot race on the track and the ominous sky. On lap 137 rain began to hit the cars. The flagman held off, hoping it would be a brief shower. But the rain came down harder and harder.

On the slippery track, a car skidded out of control

into the infield. The starter could hold off no longer, and he pulled out the checkered flag and the red flag. The next time lap leader Johnnie Parsons sped past, the starter waved both flags high, one in each hand. The race was ended.

Johnnie Parsons had won the greatest victory of his distinguished career as a race driver. Grinning and soaked, he pulled into Victory Lane for a wet celebration. Cheers rolled down from the grandstands, for Parsons was a fan favorite. Many drivers were wishing they could be so lucky as to have a cracked engine block.

As Johnnie Parsons was to do later with his son, his own father had resisted his desire to go into racing. He argued when Johnnie told him what he wanted to do with his life.

Finally his son promised, "I'll give it all up, I'll quit racing completely on the day I win the 500-mile race at Indianapolis." From a young man who had yet to make any name at all in racing, it seemed like an egotistical, far-fetched thing to promise, like a high-school hockey player promising to quit after he won the Stanley Cup.

So on that victorious day, Johnnie Parsons slipped away from the soggy celebration as soon as he could and went to a garage telephone. He placed a long-distance call to his father in California.

"Dad," he said happily, "do you remember?"

Though it had been years before, the elder Parsons answered immediately, "I sure do, son.

"I guess you've learned how to drive those cars,

Johnnie, so go ahead and drive them. If it's what you want, I'm releasing you from your promise. And congratulations, son."

Johnnie Parsons gave a great deal to auto racing. The Championship Trail was poorer on that day in 1959 when he pulled in after a practice lap and announced with a shaky voice that he was retiring from the job he loved.

Today his son, now a handsome, dark-haired carbon copy of his father, races and wins. And Johnnie, silver-haired, but still the one in the crowd who turns women's heads, advises his son from the pits.

You could even say that Johnny Parsons is luckier than many young drivers trying to make it in big-time racing, since he had two fathers to help, both of them racing champions.

Johnny's father is Indy winner Johnnie Parsons. His stepfather is Indy driver and racing champion Duane Carter, Sr. Johnny Parsons and Duane Carter, Jr., are half brothers. Duane, Sr., and Johnnie are good friends, and they both advise Johnny and Duane, Jr.

Johnny was twenty-five years old when he told Shav Glick, motor sports writer for the Los Angeles *Times*, "Both my dad and Duane discouraged me from becoming a race driver and so did my mother." In fact, Johnny first of all became a Los Angeles policeman. He had a distinguished record and citations for bravery in his brief career before retiring from the force to try his hand at racing full time.

It wasn't so much the danger of racing that caused his

Johnnie Parsons in midget race car number 1 battles with Bill "Mad Russian" Vukovich in car number 54 during a dirt-track race in the 50s. *(J. C. Agajanian photo)*

family to be negative about it with him. Auto racing is more than danger. It's tough and hard and a difficult way to make a living. Before the big purses come, if they ever do, a driver faces years of small purses or of no purses at all. Even though Johnny Parsons was the son of one great driver and the stepson of another, he still had to strap into the racer on his own. But now, Johnny told Glick in Los Angeles, "After I have finally convinced them I was going to race anyway, they all have helped. Whenever I drive out here my dad is there to help, and when I'm in the Midwest Duane looks after me."

"I've got to admit that I have mixed emotions about my son," Johnnie Parsons said. "The kid does have some ability because he's made the starting field at Indy more than once."

"I'd like him to do well because he's decided to do it. But you can get hurt there. Things fall off cars, or it's possible for someone to mess up in front of you—things you can't control.

"I talked against it for several years, but he was determined. He was an outstanding policeman, then he decided to become a pro racing driver."

Pride is obvious in the senior Parsons's voice, but worry shows, too. Johnnie Parsons wishes he could be in the cockpit with his son, not because he doesn't have confidence in him, but so that, just in case, he might be there to help the younger, less-experienced driver.

Still, Johnny does pretty well for himself, as he demonstrated at the Indianapolis Raceway Park in Claremont, Indiana, in 1975.

Johnnie Parsons celebrates his Indianapolis Speedway victory in 1950 with his wife and Wilbur Shaw. Note Parsons' wet shoulders and the raindrops on Shaw's coat. *(Indianapolis Speedway photo)*

It was a strange, oddly configured midget racer that appeared at the track that night. Midget racing cars have always tended to look the same over the years, though engines have changed. The little cars look like the old-style Indy cars, with open cockpit, down-curving tail, and long, narrow nose. That's the way they always looked, and cars that didn't look like that generally didn't do too well on the track.

This car, though, was a squat, flat, mid-engine design and looked more like a reduced version of a modern Indy car. The car, owned by Bob Lockard, was called a Badger. Nobody really expected that it would do any better than any other maverick midget race car flying in the face of tradition.

Johnny Parsons had seen something in this odd design. To him the car looked fast and durable. Besides, in 1975, he was not yet in a position to be too choosy. The car was available, he was available, so why not. He hadn't won a United States Auto Club race for over two years, and he was hungry for a victory.

As the screaming, forty-lap race began, champion Mel Kenyon grabbed the lead from pole-position holder Dana Carter, younger brother of Duane Carter, Jr., and half-brother of Johnny Parsons. Jimmy Caruthers, a fine young USAC National Midget Champion who later died of cancer, pushed into second place. Back in the field, "cooling it," as he later said, was Johnny Parsons.

From the first Parsons had seen that the mid-engine car had something extra. He could feel its willingness through the gas pedal. But racing is more than charging up through the field to take the checkered flag. The driver must handle his own car and be aware of everybody else on the track as well. As he moves up he must also stay out of trouble. A mistake by any one driver can take several other drivers out of the race, drivers who had nothing at all to do with the original problem.

Caruthers slipped around Kenyon, but on the main stretch only a few dozen yards ahead the cars of Tommy Astone and Larry Patton were spinning. Immediately the yellow flag came out and the field bunched behind Caruthers. Parsons bided his time.

Then came the break he was waiting for. Mel Kenyon slipped a little high on lap six and Johnny passed on the inside. Behind Parsons, hoping to make the same pass, was Bill Engelhart. Engelhart's wheels touched Kenyon's wheels, sending four-time midget champion Kenyon into the wall and out of the race.

By lap ten Caruthers, though Parsons was pressing him hard, was still in the lead. In third place was Engelhart. Johnny Parsons studied the situation from the cockpit of the careening little midget racer. Engelhart posed no threat. The mid-engine car could stay ahead of him. What about Caruthers? Parsons watched the speeding blue car just ahead. Then he saw what he was looking for. Although Caruthers was driving as smoothly as ever, one of his rear tires was failing. The sustained, intense driving was causing the tire to wear more than normal. Parsons knew that Jimmy Caruthers had only a limited time left.

He continued to pressure. Then it happened.

Caruther's tire could no longer bite the track. The blue racer went into a long slide through the first turn. Instantly Parsons slipped around into the lead.

By the end of the race Parsons was far in front, with Bill Engelhart second. Caruthers had finally dropped out with a sour engine. It was the first victory for Parsons in two years. It was the first victory ever for a mid-engine racer in a USAC midget race.

Some of the older fans in the stands that night watched and compared. If young Parsons would only clench a white handkerchief between his teeth as his father used to do—to protect his teeth against the brutal shaking of the car on the rutted dirt track—father and son would look much alike.

"People have said that watching me is like watching my father again," says Parsons, "but I'm not that sure. I'm learning. He was truly the best when he won the National Driving Championship and the Indy 500."

Johnny Parsons says today that he has always viewed his father and his father's racing career with a great deal of respect. "He was doing what he wanted to do and it was something that most people only wished they could do. But not many people could drive a race car well." Of his father's career, Johnny has the most vivid impression, naturally, of the 500 victory: "I was four years old then and I still remember well. He was always a front runner."

Winning the 500 at Indianapolis tops off the life and career of a driver. No matter what else he accomplishes, he is counted as a success if he wins that one single race. No matter if he winds up broke or never wins another race, he is honored in the motor-racing business for that one victory. An Indy victory is said to be worth today about $1,000,000 to the winner—$250,000 in cash on the spot, the rest in income from endorsements and personal appearances.

No son of a former winner has ever won the Indianapolis Speedway race. Some continue to try, and among them are a couple of real potentials. One is Johnny Parsons.

Buddy Baker (left) and his father, champion Buck Baker, several years
ago. (NASCAR photo)

7 BAKER

Elzie Wylie Baker, Jr., of Charlotte, North Carolina, is the biggest man in professional stock car racing and perhaps the biggest man in any kind of racing: he's six feet tall and weighs 215 pounds. Perhaps because he seems so soft-spoken and shy, people get away with calling him Buddy.

His father is Elzie Wylie Baker, Sr. He is also a race driver and they call him Buck.

NASCAR keeps a list of historic moments in NASCAR racing, a year-by-year selection of the most outstanding adventures, driving and otherwise, of the Association. Considering that NASCAR is the oldest stock car sanctioning body and the largest and strongest stock car association, getting on its historic moments list takes some doing. Some years they just skip—only the real stuff makes NASCAR's list.

Here is one entry from it:

"Labor Day, 1964, Buck Baker becomes the second man to win three Southern 500's. First two victories in 1963 and 1960."

Down a few lines is another:

"March 24, 1970. Buddy Baker becomes the first man ever to turn a closed course at 200 miles per hour, averaging 200.447 miles per hour at the Alabama International Speedway in a Dodge."

This record-making father-son combination is still going. Buck retired for a while, but he came back, and the pair was still racing in 1976.

Stock car expert Bill Dredge says of Buck and Buddy Baker, "Both drivers, at their peak, evidence the same hard-charger character. But Buddy is far more polished, a far better technician, and much more of a thinking and planning driver than his father ever was. I have to say that the son has far outstripped the father, and in this case, it was a tough act to follow. Buddy Baker is perhaps the most underrated stock car driver on the track today. With the proper equipment and another year or two of maturity, he will be just as unbeatable as Petty or Pearson.

"He's bolder and more aggressive than either man today, and seasoning will make him equally foxy. If I had to pick one man out of stock car racing to replace Richard Petty in a sponsorship, my first choice would be Buddy Baker."

Buddy Baker has never won the NASCAR Grand National Driving Championship, but Buck was champion twice, in 1956 and 1957. It was Buck who gave Buddy his first chance in a major race. With only sixteen out of an original field of forty-four still running, and with the Baker car in second place, Buddy took over Buck's car in the 1965 Darlington race, which was known among that year's fans as the Darlington Destruction Derby.

Buddy's car was one of those that dropped out of the race earlier. The entry of their two cars made Buck and Buddy one of the few father-son combinations to have competed against each other in the same race.

The finish went on Buck's great record, but the honor of crossing the finish line in that difficult race went to Buddy. Unfortunately for the Baker team, the overheating racer of Ned Jarrett managed to make it to the finish line first, even though it was clanking and banging by then. Buddy came in second, with the two cars side by side when the checkered flag fell.

Becoming a Grand National Stock Car Driving Champion is a difficult accomplishment. It is similar to winning more than once at Indianapolis, or winning the Stanley Cup in hockey.

Buck Baker was champ twice. Buddy Baker will no doubt make it in the future.

Two of Buddy Baker's greatest victories have occurred at the infamous Grand National track at Talladega, Alabama (which race drivers pronounce *TalDEEgah*). This track, Alabama International Speedway, has had a history of bizarre incidents and worse since the day Bill France built it as a second showplace for NASCAR racing. On the day it opened in 1969 the big-name drivers boycotted it as being unsafe. They said the track surface was too rough for the high speeds generated by the five-story banked turns. To

111

this day speeds are too high, beyond human control, say some drivers.

Baker won the pole position for the 1975 race with an average speed of 189.947 miles per hour. But the track lived up to its sinister reputation as the race thundered on.

That day Richard Petty's brother-in-law was killed in a freak accident in the pits. Richard smoked in with a burning wheel bearing. Each pit at Talladega has a pressurized water tank with a spray hose. It was the job of Randy Owens, brother of Richard's wife and a member of the family-oriented Petty Engineering organization, to spray water on the bearing to cool it down during the pit stop. As he reached over the tank to turn on the pressure, it suddenly exploded, hurling the twenty-one-year-old more than thirty feet into the air. Several others were hurt. Young Owens was killed. Petty, who was not hurt, withdrew from the race.

On the track, trying to break his personal Talladega jinx, was Buddy Baker. Twice before he had started at the track on the pole, and twice before he had lost the race. Buddy Baker had a long reputation in NASCAR for allowing his foot to command his brain—for being much too hard on his equipment and for driving flat out every mile of the way. But he had not won a major race in more than two years.

Every driver that day was mindful of the string of sad events at the track. Although it was the fastest speedway on the entire NASCAR circuit, it was developing an ominous reputation. Larry Smith was killed there in 1973 in a single-car crash. The same year a wild nineteen-car crash was the worst in NASCAR history for the number of racers involved. At least that time there were no fatalities.

In 1974 a member of the Penske crew lost his leg when he was caught between the pit wall and the Matador of Penske driver Gary Bettenhausen. The Penske crew had been servicing the Matador when another car rammed it, shoving it into the wall.

As the 1975 Talladega race drew near the end, it had become a two-car battle between Baker and David Pearson. With only three laps to go, they were bumper-to-bumper. The crowd was standing, waving and cheering them on. Baker knew that Pearson might try to slingshot him on the last lap.

Sure enough, on the fourth turn of the last lap, Baker drifted high to prevent Pearson from blasting around on the outside. Pearson had to back off or hit the wall. With only seconds to go he squirmed down to the inside, and it appeared for an instant that he might straighten out and pass Baker. But his front fender was beside the driver's door of Baker's car as the two flashed across the finish line.

They asked Pearson later if he thought his strategy of waiting until the last lap to pass was best.

"It must not have been," he answered dryly. "I lost."

Was Baker's strategy in blocking him high up on the track good?

"It must have been. He won."

Would Pearson have done the same if the situation had been reversed?

"Yeah, I sure would have."

Baker was interviewed in his garage after this close finish. Often called the Gentle Giant, he is soft-spoken and retiring.

"I saw the checkered flag and I said, 'Lord, don't let it fall until I get there. He's had it fall on him here before, and I haven't. Now it's my turn.' I guess the Lord heard me; I was saying it loud enough."

Buddy Baker had broken his own Talladega jinx by winning in 1975. Once broken, it seemed smashed forever. He won the next race at the same track the same year. This time he beat Richard Petty by a scant three feet, though Baker's car was low on oil pressure and struggling for the finish line. It was another of those exciting NASCAR finishes so pleasing to stock car fans.

But the overall Talladega jinx continued. During that race, there was a terrible crash that took the life of Tiny Lund, a popular driver and great pal of Baker's.

Grand National stock car drivers are a unique breed of men, and Buddy Baker is a perfect example. They are folksy, down-home types, active in community affairs and generally churchgoers. They like people to call them by their first name. Unlike the perhaps more worldly, high-living drivers in other types of racing, southern stock car drivers try to take their wives and families to the track. They often have family members serving on their pit crews.

Their fans love them and speak fondly of Richard, Buddy, or Cale, whom they think of as just-down-the-road neighbors.

Almost all these "good ol' boys" are small-town

Buddy Baker's car makes a Grand National pit stop during a 125-mile Daytona race in 1973. *(NASCAR photo)*

people, coming from places like Horseshoe, Asheville, Timmonsville, Level Cross, Hueytown, and Ellerbe. Few finished high school, and fewer still attended college. They are easy to like, although they often stiffen up around anybody but another southerner.

Though it is hard to tell from talking to them or watching them, many of them are very rich indeed.

Just as Buddy Baker typifies the southern stock car driver, his car is a good example of the custom that keeps professional auto racing going—sponsorship. The sponsors, much more than the ticket-buying public, provide the funds necessary for the sport. Racing cars are high-speed billboards with sponsors' names strategically placed and sized according to their financial investment in the team. On the side of Buddy Baker's car are the names of many companies, each of which provides services, parts, or money to hold the team together.

"Union 76," it says in bold letters. "Champion" helps the team out, and so do "Hurst," "Regal Ride," "Purolator," "Grey Rock," "Winston," and "Goodyear."

Most of these companies also sponsor many other cars in the same race, and some are involved with all the cars. Last-minute deals occasionally send company representatives scurrying about the grid moments before a big race, plastering new decals on cars.

One name overshadows all others on Baker's stock car. Front, rear, and sides are all filled with a big circle with the letters *NI* and the name NORRIS. Companies having nothing to do with racing or cars sponsor race cars; decals with the names of cosmetics, beers, and cigarettes are often seen. Norris Industries, NI, makes toilet bowls. It also makes ovens, garbage disposals, and other household products.

How does a toilet-bowl maker get into auto racing? Years ago a young amateur racer was seeking a company to help him financially. He knocked on the door at Norris Industries at exactly the right time.

"He probably looked us up in the Yellow Pages," says Ken Norris, president of the company, "but in 1970 we decided that auto racing represented a technically allied medium through which we could tell the story of our company and its products and capabilities. Since then, the Norris banner has raced on virtually every major circuit in North America."

That's the key, the telling of "the story of the company and its products."

This kind of storytelling doesn't come cheap. It costs $150,000 and up per year to sponsor a stock car on the Grand National circuit, and more than $350,000 for a USAC team with a major driver.

Ken Norris arranged the company's first major sponsorship for the inaugural California 500 at the Ontario Motor Speedway in 1970. As the cars were being pushed to the line for the start, painters were still lettering the name NORRIS on the side of LeRoy Yarbrough's Brabham racer.

What happened? Al Unser led most of the race, then Peter Revson took over when Al's car failed. But Revson's car wouldn't start after a pit stop, so he was out. And who was then in the lead? From out of nowhere it seemed the "good ol' boy" from the southern stock car circuit, LeRoy Yarborough, was in the lead and pulling away. LeRoy appeared certain to win the most talked-about, widely seen race in many years. On the side of his racer, just drying, was the huge blue NORRIS sign for all to see.

Up in one of the luxury sponsors' suites Ken Norris pointed at the leader with a smile and a cheer as he flashed by on the track below.

Ken Norris never points at his racers now. At that very instant the engine of Yarborough's car blew into a million pieces in a great white cloud of smoke. He didn't even make it through the first turn. Jim McElreath won the race while they were towing LeRoy through the infield back to the garage.

Still, Ken Norris had obtained for his company what he was paying for. Even though it would have been nice to bask in Victory Circle at the Big O with everybody taking pictures, a Norris car had led, and that would do until a Norris car won. The company continued to pour money into auto racing, but it was years before the first great victory.

That also happened at the Big O at Ontario, California. This time Norris got his turn in Victory Circle, which, for the nostalgic race fan, is a circle of bricks removed from the "brickyard," the Indianapolis Motor Speedway, when they paved the place.

That day in 1975 was hot, dry, and clear at the Ontario Motor Speedway. The track had been built at

It's Petty leading Baker at the Big O at Ontario, California, but Buddy Baker came on to win the race after 500 grueling miles. *(Author)*

tremendous cost to include every possible feature to make the fans comfortable and the racing the best. For example, the infield is down a few feet in a gigantic hole so that the entire two-and-one-half-mile track can be seen from anywhere in the grandstand. The track struggled on for years to make its cost pay off to investors.

Despite its financial woes, the Big O was a beautiful setting for a 1975 NASCAR stock car race on an oval track. The more traditional track for this type of racing is a high-banked, tri-oval design, not a nearly flat track like Ontario.

If it had not been for the last-minute sponsorship of Norris Industries for the Ontario race, Baker would have been doing what he loves next best, "fishin' for striped bass" back home on the Santee Cooper Lake in South Carolina, jawing with his neighbors about crops, weather, and the best bait.

Instead, he was on the starting line at Ontario in his blue-and-white Bud Moore-prepared 1976 Dodge. One month before, Baker had won the Dixie 500 at Atlanta, Georgia, in the same car. But it was Richard Petty, as always, who was favored in the Los Angeles *Times* 500 at Ontario. Petty is favored anywhere and anytime he races.

Baker had started racing in 1959, and in 1975 he was having his finest season. Already he had won three Grand National races that year. He may have been surprised to be off the lake and on the grid at Ontario, but he was ready to go. He had qualified his car for a front-row spot for the flying start. He was confident. He was almost glad to be away from the peace and quiet of Santee Cooper and into the hectic, colorful mass of people and cars that is a Grand National grid.

Baker really drove up a storm in the race that year. For five hundred miles he battled for the lead. Car after car either dropped out with mechanical problems or spun out and hit the wall. Baker charged on. In all, he led 149 laps of the total of 200. At one point in the great race there was a seven-car drafting train, bumper-to-bumper, with drivers Baker, Allison, Yarborough, Foyt, Petty, Pearson, and Marcis delicately holding position against each other, using each other. Baker's hands were blistered and starting to bleed.

At the end he was more than twenty-nine seconds ahead of Pearson, who finished in second place.

Nearly out of gas, not even taking an extra cool-down lap for fear of having to walk back, Baker met his sponsor Ken Norris in Victory Circle. After years of sponsorship, it was Norris's first time. He was elated.

Baker was himself, smiling but subdued. He accepted a check for over $31,000, along with the keys to a brand-new Datsun sports car, for his three and a half hours of work. He smiled through the photo session.

"Turn this way, Buddy!"

"Over here, Buddy."

"Wave, wave."

"OK, now kiss the queen, Buddy . . . "

"Ken, give Buddy a kiss!"

Buddy Baker (right) with Coo Coo Marlin, after a victory in a 125-mile Daytona race in 1973. (*NASCAR photo*)

"Take off the cap!"

"Put on the cap. Look this way. Now shake hands with Bud Moore. Wave buddy wave!"

Buddy waved, smiled, posed, and kissed all those he was asked to kiss, but through it all you got the idea that he was a race car driver who considered it all just part of the job. Then he confirmed what you knew all along.

"I'll be back on the lake tomorrow," he said softly. "I hope I didn't miss any of the big ones."

Maybe that's what it's really all about.

INDEX

INDEX

Index

The Author

Racing authority Ross R. Olney has written several books for Putnam's including *Superstars of Auto Racing, The Racing Bugs: Formula Vee and Super Vee, Kings of the Dragstrips, Kings of Motor Speed,* and *Great Dragging Wagons.* An authority on other sports as well, he has also written *Kings of the Surf* and the recent *Hang Gliding.* Mr. Olney, who likes to race cars, skin-dive, and sail, lives with his wife and three children in Ventura, California.